peace

this book belongs to:

To my magnificent daughters,
Blair and Jordan,
who inspire me to reach for my highest self every day.
~ Your Mom

TRISTAN Publishing, Inc.
2355 Louisiana Avenue North
Golden Valley, MN 55427

Copyright © 2012, Joan Steffend
ISBN 978-0-931674-57-0
First Printing
Printed in China

To learn about all of our books with a message please visit
www.TRISTANpublishing.com

peace in peace out

by joan steffend and you

TRISTAN PUBLISHING
Minneapolis

welcome

We have been given one tool to change the world, and it is our magnificent self. This book invites you to collaborate on peaceful ideas with me.

The first half offers some of my thoughts about reclaiming peace in yourself and then offering peace and kindness to the world, in the simplest of ways.

The second half is for you and your brilliance.

I believe we are all connected and what we do, say, think, and believe affects us all, so I love that we get to write this book together.

I sit here in this moment and think, what do I have to offer the world regarding inner peace? Who am I to write a book on the subject?
I have lived a life in search of peace...and fallen short much of the time.
Maybe that's exactly why I get to write the book.
I don't live on a mountaintop of perfected bliss.

I live in the world – the messy, chaotic, confounding world. I lift myself up and I have a crazy tendency to fall back down, always hoping to be slightly wiser, slightly more loving and slightly more peaceful.

So what follows this confession is information from the spiraling path I've been living the past few decades. Some suggestions may resonate with you and some may not.

That is perfect.

You get to decide what has real meaning for you and how to navigate your path.
Not me.
Still, there may be places where we are alike enough that I can offer a sense of direction.
If that is so,
I am grateful.
And in this moment...
I am peaceful.

peace in

First thing in the morning...smile...at yourself. I know a lot of first moments are spent in the agony of the alarm clock, but you're getting up one way or the other, so you may as well start off with energy that sets a better tone for your day. Take a deep breath. Stretch. Smile. Smile in bed. Smile at your bed-head self in the mirror. Think of a reason to smile.

peace out

You can see this one coming.

Smile at someone else – a real one. Not one of those grimaces we've decided can pass for a smile out on the street. Show some teeth and put a twinkle in it, for goodness' sake! To be honest, some people may look at you like you're crazy, but your job is to offer the good energy. If it doesn't come back from that person...it'll come back to you in another way.

peace in

Spend time in your childhood.
What did you love to do before you turned into an "adult?" Take things apart? Paint? Dream of flying? Perform? Teach a class filled with neighborhood kids?
Excavate a little and see where you've put that part of yourself. See if you can find a place for that part of you in your grownup life. It might be a hobby. It might be a career change. It might be writing a book on peace.

peace out

Put away the usual topics of conversation for a day and ask someone else about the dreams they had as a child. If your experience is anything like mine, you will see an adult transform into a seven year old in no time! Encourage them to reconnect with their child-like spirit. The world can look pretty magical again from a seven year old's perspective.

peace in

What do you say when you pass a mirror? Have you ever listened to what you say to yourself? Most of the time, it isn't pretty. We oughta be a) taller b) smarter c) lighter d) all of the above in order to be acceptable. Just for today (and then maybe tomorrow), be aware of what you are filling your head with. Just take notice. If you can, write some of your "self talk" down so you can see what kind of friend you are to your brilliant self.

peace out

Walk through a crowd of people, sit at your desk, or watch TV, and see how often you find reasons to criticize the folks in your world. Make a mental note of how many times you send the "too" message out. You know, too fat...too thin...too pretty...too confident... too smart...dressed too weird...driving too slow... driving too fast...too different from me.

The message is received whether you say it out loud or not.

Today...be aware of your mental relationship with other people who you know and who you don't know.

peace in

When I was young, I was an explorer. I'd leave the house on a summer morning and only come back for meals. I looked for new experiences and figured out who I was in the middle of them.
If you are living a life now that feels more like a rut than an adventure, look for small ways to see your world and yourself in a new way. Take a different way to work. After work, stop in a park you've never been to before and see what new things there are to see! Look at your hometown through the eyes of an explorer.

peace out

There are people you pass every day and don't think a thing of it. Start a conversation with one. Every single person you pass has a story. Every single person has a spark of wisdom and joy in them that they may be willing to share with you (or not, but that is an adventure, too).

peace in

Look at yourself with the eyes of an explorer! Imagine that you just met you. What are your first impressions? What do you communicate? Are you open for conversation? Closed to the business of really meeting someone? Are you meeting the world with the air of someone who sees new people with curiosity or is it closer to indifference? The choice is yours.

peace out

Now think about that practice with the people closest to you – spouses, partners, children, friends. After you've decided what another person is all about, quite often we put that judgment into concrete and don't allow them to grow out of it. Put on a fresh pair of "glasses" today. Make it a day of "first meetings" with those you love.

peace in

Did you choose this book because you liked its cover?

Well, we worked hard on it, so thank you, but you've spent a good share of your life being judged by your cover. Can you let the fear of not looking good enough go for even one day? I like to imagine a world with no mirrors and no reflective surfaces – where all we have to connect to others is our authentic nature. We spend a lot more time dressing and polishing up our outside than we do embracing and offering up our best inside. Consider flipping that today.

peace out

My imagination can get the better of me. I can look at a person driving by in a car and imagine their whole life – personality included. I do it with people I meet in business and social settings, too. I put them in the box they seem best suited for. I might discount them or open up a big old line of credit for them, depending on how they look. I am quite often mistaken. Open up your heart to someone's interior design and stop pretending you're a guest judge on a fashion show.

peace in

I just came back from laying in my backyard.
I just couldn't resist spending some time
looking at the sky, supported by the earth.
Remember doing that as a kid? I remember
it mostly from ice skating season – being
so tired from balancing on those blades
that I'd collapse on the snow bank and feel
the stillness and the big-ness of it all. The
mystery was present and so was I.
I stopped for decades.
It's good to be back.
Try it.

peace out

Sharing doesn't only need to be with people. I have to say that when I look into my dog Charlie's eyes and try to show him how important he is to me, it just comes back like a big old boomerang.

It automatically turns the peace out back into a peace in.

It's heavenly.

It's a model for living we don't see as much outside of the animal world – that easy unconditional circle of love and adoration.

Show animals love.

peace in

This may feel a little esoteric to some of you, but try it anyway.

Bring yourself back to a memory you have as a child or as an adult, where you felt connected to something greater than yourself or where peace was present. Really feel it – smells, sight, sounds.

Use that expansive and peaceful moment as a touchstone in your day. Bring yourself back there as often as you can and see how it shapes your day.

peace out

If someone brings stress into your day, be still for a moment. I have been known to build a big, daunting defense in a millisecond when it feels like an offense is coming at me. That can create a stalemate that no one wins. A moment (or ten) can give you the space to see if a response will get you to a better place or not. We don't have control over the other person. We do have control over how we react to them.

peace in

What would you do today if no one was watching and no one was judging? Would you sing in your car – and not just when the lane next to you was empty? Would you wear mis-matched multi-colored socks with your business suit? Would you roll in the newly raked leaves in your front yard – no matter who was peeking out their window? Would you revel in the smallest act of rebellion?
I dare you.

peace out

Here's the deal. When you dare to do something that is slightly outside the norm… you give permission to others to do the same. There's a freedom in not being the perfect definition of a grownup every hour of every day. Give someone else that gift, by showing them who you are!

peace in

This one crept up on me in my car the other day. I was feeling kind of low and a love song came on the radio. Something inside of me decided to listen to that song as if I was singing it to myself. It felt great! I searched for another love song and did the same...and then maybe a few times more. Why shouldn't we remind ourselves that we're worth a love song?

peace out

I'm not given to huge blanket statements very often, but I'm absolutely positive I agree with me 100% on this one: Everyone wants to be loved. The smallest word or act of encouragement from you may be the only love someone gets today. Look for those opportunities. It is such a small act of compassion and one that everyone can afford. It can literally change someone's life, including yours.

peace in

This is my favorite question! I would put this question on every page of this book if I could! It is the question I ask myself when I'm frustrated or in the middle of an argument or feeling like a victim. It immediately takes me from my unhappy head to my open heart.
It is a simple question:
What would peace feel like in this moment?
That's it.
I hope it has magic for you, too.

peace out

Well, if I can't have it on every page, I can at least have it on two pages, right?

I invite you to tape this question to your car dashboard or inside your desk drawer at work, since there seems to be a fair amount of irritation on the freeway or inside office buildings. It'll be a great reminder that you have a choice in how you react – drama or peace.

peace in

Breathe.

Ha! I'll bet you're already doing this a dozen times a minute or so, but I'm inviting you to find some trigger in your environment that will remind you to stop, look, listen and breathe more consciously.

A friend of mine suggested taking that moment of mindfulness and oxygen every time you are at a red light. You could set your phone alarm to alert you once, twice, three times a day. Stress could remind you.

That moment of inhale and exhale takes you out of the mindlessness and reminds you who is doing the breathing.

peace out

We've all been in situations where we see someone in need, but can't do anything about it. Maybe it was a homeless person you saw on the streets as you were driving. Maybe it's someone you know making consistent choices that seem to be hurting them. If you watch the news, it is filled with stories of need and tragedy that can fill you with a sense of helplessness.

Try offering up a moment of peace, asking for what is in their best interest. Inhale mindfully and exhale a hope of peace and healing for them, without judgment as to what that looks like. I'm not saying that action and physical assistance doesn't have its wonderful place. I'm saying that your kind intentions carry weight too.

peace in

In my mind, nature is a teacher, a healer, and a path to loving your amazing self. Spend time with it.

I've said this in public before, and people will say that they don't have access to nature, but I'm not talking about ocean waves crashing on an island coast or a mountain view or even a lakeshore cottage. I'm talking the intricacies of a dandelion, the perfection of an orange, the absolute miracle of your body (Look Ma, no batteries!).

Nature offers up a beautiful lesson of being with no anxious striving. There appears to be a plan in nature. You are part of nature. What plan could you be waking up to?

peace out

Point out beauty to others when you see it.
Sometimes it seems like our most common
conversations with others revolve around weather
– specifically weather complaints. We can move
quickly from "it's too cold" to "it's too hot" without
any stop at "it's just right." Add in a weekend
thunderstorm or a snowfall you need to shovel
and you could talk for hours!
We can so easily ignore the blazing sunset or
the beauty of the snowfall or the gift of the
thunderstorm. Why complain about what we can't
control? Choose to see the beauty and to share it.

peace in

Silence.
Look for the opportunity to be alone with yourself. Quite often, we're surrounded by people, chatted up by the radio station, entertained by the TV or computer, and all around distracted from ourselves.
Silence can be a door that leads you back.
Try driving with the radio off. Go sit on a park bench. Have a conversation with yourself. See what you're thinking and feeling these days!

peace out

Find a place for silence in your relationships.
This could be a hard one.

I was always someone who needed to fill every silence with conversation. I couldn't get comfortable enough with friends to just be quiet. I thought I needed to entertain to be liked! I've developed a greater appreciation for silence. I recently gathered around a bonfire with twenty-five people, mostly standing silently. I felt connected to each one of them and never said a word.

peace in

Meditate!
I know I just scared some of you and I apologize.
I'm not suggesting a half-day marathon of
pretzel poses. I am thinking more like a few
minutes here and a few minutes there of
emptying your mind.
Quiet your thoughts by focusing on your
breathing, or repeating a beautiful word in your
mind, or staring at a candle flame. If thoughts
intrude, don't let that frustrate you, just re-
focus as often as you need.
It's like learning a foreign language. It takes time,
but it makes the trip more meaningful.

peace out

Walk down the street and really see everyone
you pass by. See them and offer them a kind
thought. Entertain yourself with it! Don't offer
everyone the same thought. Your imagination
needs a workout just like your body. Imagine
all the opportunities for gifting people with all
kinds of kind thoughts!

peace in

I think it's time for a break.
The culture has been telling you since you were born, that you need to compete and work harder than everyone else in order to achieve success.
I have no problem with working passionately, but even working passionately, you need time to relax and recharge and fill your cup. It's not a want. It's a need if you're going to contribute your best and live a conscious loving life.
Give yourself a break. Listen to what your career needs and listen to what you need.
Strike a balance today.

peace out

Take off the judge's robes.
Give someone else a break today, too.
Everybody's human. Everybody has issues.
Everybody makes mistakes.
Everybody.

peace in

I am magnificent.
You heard me.
I am magnificent and so are you.
Start your day and end your day with words
that tell you who you are on your best day
and in your best life.

peace out

Look...really look for the magnificence in someone else.
We have been a culture that seems to delight in being more magnificent than someone else.
Let's call it a tie.

peace in

Forgive yourself.
Expect that you will do well today, but don't beat yourself up if the day falls a little short of rock star status.
The best lessons sometimes arrive in prickly looking packages. Look for the lesson, and spend less time on the pain.
When you accept the lesson, that particular package may stop arriving at your door.

peace out

Forgive someone their differences.
I was an ace speller in junior high school and I used
that as a reason to convict people in my mind of
some felony spelling offense. Weird, I know.
But sometimes, when we know what is "right," we use
it as a reason to make someone else "wrong."
If you've memorized every rule about etiquette, that's
great. You can still forgive the person who hasn't.

peace in

Pick a word.
Pick a word for the day, the week, the month, or the year.
Make it a good one, because that word becomes a touchstone that keeps pulling you back to an ideal for yourself.
I used to choose words for a year at a time. Be. That was a good one, but my all-time favorite is peace.

peace out

Words are powerful.
They carry an energy that sticks to people.
The hope here is that you weigh your words carefully. Take that deep breath and feel how they'll be received before speaking them.

peace in

Know that you are a unique and perfect puzzle piece of the universe.

peace out

Remind yourself that if you are, then who is not?

peace in

You are a magnet.
Notice what you are attracting.
If you don't like what you see, ask yourself what you might be able to change in hopes of a different outcome.
Imagine wonderful people and experiences being drawn to you.
Why not?

peace out

Look into the eyes of a child who you know and tell them how amazing they are. Tell them about their potential. We are all gifted, but are sometimes led to believe it has to be a certain kind of gift in order to be acceptable.

They may remember your acceptance and kindness for their whole life.

You, my friend, have just shaped the future.

peace in

Think about a family story told about you, one
that has defined you in the family and in your life.
Ask yourself if it was true then and if it is true now.
Give yourself the option of dropping that story.
You may have outgrown it as easily as you outgrew
your clothes from childhood.
If you have, don't waste any more energy on it.
Don't let the old stories keep you from writing
your best life story today.

peace out

Ask the children in your life who they are
and what they love. Believe them.
Offer them assistance in hanging on to
what makes them special.
They come complete with wisdom and
talent and personality.
In this world, they often need a little
encouragement to hold on to that.

peace in

I invite you to take a minute in the morning and a minute at night and list what you are grateful for.
I figure if you are not grateful for the gifts you have, why would you get more?
Even in the worst of times in my life, my list has taken more than a minute.
I am grateful for that.

peace out

What gets created?
This is another cool question that can keep me closer to a peaceful place.
When times get stressful and you're tempted to lash out or get something off your chest, take a moment and ask yourself, "What gets created if I do this?"
You may still go ahead and speak your truth, but it will be done with an eye on its purpose.

peace in

We all know that music has a magic of its own and certain songs have a way of creeping into your consciousness, wanted or not.

Well, consider choosing a song that carries the energy of the day you'd like to have and use that as your reminder during the day.

You don't need to sing it out loud, but why not?

peace out

You may decide to share your song only after you've achieved perfection, but that wouldn't be as much fun! Be vulnerable today.

I'm not a big fan of glossy perfection. I always say that, if you offer the world too smooth and polished a surface, there's nothing for anyone to grab on to.

Humans tend to really connect at the broken places. The conversations that sound more like "That happens to you, too?" rather than "That's a beautiful suit."

Admit a social imperfection or two. We've all got 'em.

peace in

Live in the question.
Answers are great, but there's no room for growth or movement.
Remember the old "world is flat" answer?
When you find yourself offering up absolutes in conversation, without room for exploration,
look for the key that opens your mind.
Curiosity leads you to new places.

peace out

Listen.

Instead of trying to think of the next thing you're going to say in a conversation, try actively listening to what the other is saying.

If you want someone to understand your perspective, try to understand theirs.

peace in

Adjust your rear view mirror and your attitude.
A lot of us check out and go on auto pilot
when we drive.
Try using your first moment behind the wheel
to buckle up and choose how you're going to
react on the road.
Expect that you will be relaxed, safe, and arrive
on time.
There's nothing to lose but the habitual
frustration.

peace out

Okay, now they've gone and done it.

That driver in the blue truck just cut you off!

Take a split second and remember that you have a choice.

You can let the blood boil and unpack your angry face...or you could take a breath and bless them (you heard me ☺).

You choose the first, and you'll likely carry that energy into the rest of your day.

You choose the latter and...well...you feel the difference.

Your choice.

peace in

If you yearn for something more in your life, quite often your life opens doors for you.
Look for them.
Synchronicities and coincidences might be the language your life uses to get your attention.
Your interest and excitement in a class, a book, a seminar, or anything might be another way.
Pay attention and walk through those doors.
Your life is not over or you wouldn't be reading this.

peace out

Share the possibilities of life with others.
If you complain, you get more to complain about.
If you talk and dream about passion for something wonderful, I believe the hope and imagination will take you to a better place.
It's certainly a more fun conversation.
Spend time with the dreamers.
If you're a dreamer, people will want to spend time around you.

peace in

I have an amazing mirror in my house.
Maybe it's the lighting or the angle, but I always look good in that mirror.
Choose your mirrors wisely – both the glass ones and the people in your life.
Listen to the ones who reflect your possibilities, your joy, your highest nature.
There's nothing like a good mirror.

peace out

Some mirrors aren't so great...more like a carnival fun house mirror!

If there are people in your life who insist on reflecting back the worst to you, bless them, and stop looking at them to tell you who you are.

It doesn't serve them either to spend time looking for your flaws.

peace in

When you're feeling a little low, put your hand
over your heart and ask to feel your own love.
I swear I can feel my heart open.
I expect yours will, too.

peace out

Respect the hearts of others.
Plato once said, "Be kind, for everyone you
meet is fighting a hard battle."
Choose to see the vulnerable hearts in others
and send them love.

peace in

Yes!
Say yes, and put an exclamation point on it!
Say yes to something you've been dreaming
about—a small step or if you're really daring,
a giant leap!
The world makes forward progress when
you say yes to dreams!

peace out

"No" is one of the first words we learn as kids. It's a word that keeps us safe sometimes, but it can also be a habit that leaves us predictable and stuck.

Give someone the gift today of "yes!"

peace in

Remember who you are.
Be who you are.

peace out

Share who you are.
Change the world.

now it's your turn

There is a journey to go on in this life and I think the most powerful destination is not a country... not a lifestyle...not a bank account, but knowing and loving yourself.

I invite you to use the following journal pages in any way that serves you, but if you need a little nudge, here's what I'd say:

Don't judge yourself! Write what your heart says and not what you think it should be saying. Doodle like it's nobody's business! If you want to use the rest of the book to write yourself a love story or offer blessings for others, that's perfect.

You can keep track of kindnesses given to you and the smiles you've traded with others. Make lists of dreams from long ago and today. Scribble inspiring words you may need to hear again someday.

And then, when the most authentic you starts to resonate out from these pages and in your life, you'll be delighted at the way the world rises up to love you, and so will I.

Much peace and gratitude for me and for you,

Joan

peace

peace

peace

peace

peace

peace

peace

peace

peace

peace

peace

peace

peace

peace

peace

peace

peace

peace

peace

peace

peace

peace

peace

peace

peace

peace

peace

peace

peace

peace

peace

peace

peace

peace

peace

peace

peace

peace

peace

peace

peace

peace

peace

peace

peace

peace

peace

peace

peace

peace

peace

peace

peace

peace

peace

peace

peace

peace

peace

peace

peace

peace

peace

peace

peace

peace

peace

peace

peace

peace

peace

peace

peace

peace

peace

peace

peace

peace

peace

peace

peace

peace

peace

peace

peace

Joan Steffend is a dreamer. She has had dreams fulfilled, raising two wonderful daughters, being married to a great guy, working for years on local and national TV and radio, but the grandest dream is one of inner peace and connection to a kinder world. That led her to co-found "peace begins with me" (a small BIG peace project) and to write this book.

me

peace

peace